It's not about how smart you can be.
It's about how wealthy you can be.

It's not about how smart you can be. It's about how wealthy you can be.

MAKE THE MOST OF THE MARKET

MARK VARDER
JOOST HULSBOSCH

First published by Jacana Media (Pty) Ltd in 2008

10 Orange Street
Sunnyside
Auckland Park 2092
South Africa
+2711 628 3200
www.jacana.co.za

ISBN 978-1-77009-595-3

Design and layout: Joost Hulsbosch
Printer: Tien Wah Press, Singapore
Job No. 000791

See a complete list of Jacana titles at www.jacana.co.za

R25,243.18

Now imagine you had invested R1,000 every month for the past 20 years. What would you be worth today?

R1,767,207.90

Most people think you have to be smart to make money on the stock market.

You must know which shares to buy. And when to buy them.

You must be able to pick the best performing funds.

You must understand phrases like ... err ... market fundamentals.

The smarter you are, the more money you'll make.

NO

The truth about the stock market is different. It's not about being smart. Being smart will, in fact, count against you.

Making the most of the market is breathtakingly simple. It can be explained in a few pages. In a few sentences, even.

The only difficult thing is convincing you that it is this simple.

FIRST THINGS FIRST

The contents

THE POWER OF OWNERSHIP

Look around you.

At the wealth and prosperity. At the cities, the skyscrapers, the technology, the air travel, the cars, the homes, the luxury goods.

It was not always like this. 100 years ago only a handful of people could call themselves wealthy. The Rockefellers of the world. The rest of us were the other fellows. Employees, but not owners.

Ownership is at the heart of capitalism. The reason you see a wealthy world around you is because political and economic ownership is no longer confined to kings, dictators and industrial magnates.

It has become democratised. Millions and millions of people enjoy the power of ownership.

Political ownership is your right. But how much economic ownership you enjoy is up to you.

The miracle of the stock market.

Today, thanks to Exchange Traded Funds, anyone with a few hundred Rand can become part of the vast wealth-generation of the country's economy.

This is the miracle of the stock market.

The stock market is *not* about owning shares. The stock market is about ownership, *through* shares, of the best companies in the country.

South Africa's gold, platinum and coal mines. The manufacturing and industrial giants. The cellphone companies. The huge construction companies. The banks and insurance companies. Forestry, medical and media companies. The world's biggest paper company. One of the world's biggest brewers.

The success of these companies is the reason why South Africa's stock market has doubled in value every 4 years 2 months on average for the last 20 years.

Money invested in the stock market has, on average, doubled every 4 years 2 months.

HERE'S THE POWER OF THAT OWNERSHIP

Property has, on average, doubled every 5 years 5 months.

Bonds have, on average, doubled your money every 7 years 10 months.

Inflation has, on average, doubled prices every 8 years 7 months.

Money in the bank has, on average, doubled every 9 years 8 months.

The stock market.

How many pension funds have invested money on behalf of their clients as solidly as this?

How many unit trust managers have produced a return as remarkable as this?

How many individual investors have created wealth on this scale like this?

Very few.

Yet it is possible for you to generate this sort of wealth. Provided you don't get smart.

Q.

How can you use the stock market to generate wealth like this?

It's ridiculously simple.

Exchange Traded Funds (ETFs). Ownership made simple. And cheap.

Every stock market in the world has indices (indexes) made up of its largest, most powerful, most traded companies.

Index funds make it possible for you to own all those companies with a simple investment.

Now Exchange Traded Funds take index funds one step further. They are index ***funds*** that are ***traded*** on the stock ***exchange***. When the stock market goes up, the index goes up and an ETF will rise in value. When the stock market falls, the index falls and an ETF declines in value.

ETFs let you own a wide diversity of wealth-generating companies – and they make it as simple and as cheap as buying a single share.

The world's first Exchange Traded Fund was created in 1992. It lets people own all 500 companies in America's S&P 500 index.

Every stock market in the world has its equivalent index. In Japan, it's the Nikkei Stock Average, made up of the 225 most powerful companies. In the UK, it's the FTSE 100 Index and in Mexico, the Bolsa Index.

In South Africa, we have the FTSE/JSE Top 40 index, made up of the 40 largest, most powerful, most traded companies on the South African stock exchange.

If Exchange Traded Funds had existed in South Africa 20 years ago and had you invested R1,000 a month for the past 20 years in the ETF tracking South Africa's Top 40 index ... then your personal wealth, before investment costs, would now be close to that astonishing amount on page 7.

R1,767,207.90

Exchange Traded Funds finally make simple what experts have known for a long, long time. (Since 1933.)

The way to make the most of the market is to own as much of it as possible, as cheaply as possible, for as long as possible.

Now comes the hard part. Convincing you that it really is this simple.

THE MARKET YOU KNOW AND FEAR

2

How dare you?!

It's the place you can lose a lot of money!

You have spent years earning money. Month by month, salary cheque by salary cheque. It's required dedication, but it's been steady and reliable.

The stock market looks different. With very little effort, it seems, you can create island-buying, sports car-collecting, retire-now wealth. Or, in the space of a few uncontrollable, mind-numbing hours, you can end up with nothing.

Putting money into the stock market feels unreliable, unpredictable and even irresponsible.

Up, down, strong, weak, buy, sell ...

You hear about the stock market on the radio incessantly. You see headlines all the time. You read about it in every newspaper and magazine. Experts make predictions. Commentators pick shares. Analysts plot graphs and trend lines. Everyone has an opinion.

So many things seem to affect the stock market. The gold price, the dollar, politics, the economic outlook, interest rates, unexpected global disasters.

Is this any place to invest your carefully earned money?

This bedlam is caused by speculators, trading constantly, hoping to make a quick buck in a short space of time.

Relax.

This book is not about speculators. It's not about trying to outdo the stock market.

Except for the next 26 pages.

HOW TO MAKE *LESS* OF THE MARKET

3

If for some strange reason you deliberately chose to make less – perhaps even considerably less – than the market over a 20-year period, how would you go about it?

Simple.

You would use one of the usual ways to invest in the stock market. You would try to be smart.

YOU WOULD THINK THESE ARE THE REALLY SMART WAYS TO CREATE WEALTH ON THE STOCK MARKET.

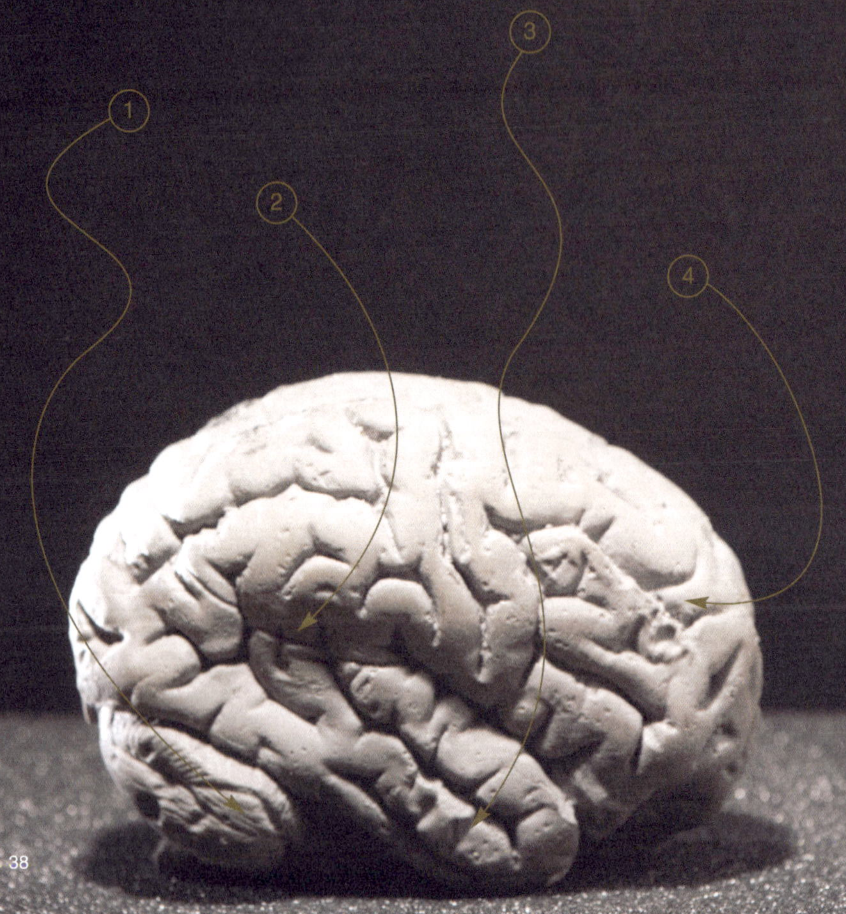

1. Time your investing

Buy only when the market is low, sell only when it's high. That's obvious.

2. Buy only the shares that will go up

That's a no-brainer. Why would anyone want to invest in shares that are going to do badly?

3. Consult an advisor or a stockbroker

These people eat, sleep and breathe the market. Use their expertise. Pay their fees. It's worth it.

4. Put your money in a unit trust

The best of two worlds. You reduce your risk by diversifying your investment - and if anyone can beat the market, it's a fund manager, right?

1. The reality of trying to time your investing?

YOU'LL EXPERIENCE THAT HORRIBLE EMPTY FEELING. OF ALWAYS BEING TOO LATE.

Only if you get your timing correct 70% of the time - an unlikely track record - will you make as much as simply buying and holding your shares.

Why is that? Simple. In the long run, the money you make when the market goes up will be more than the money you lose when the market dips.

Holding onto your shares while the market fluctuates works far better in the long run than trying to buy low and sell high.

As you'll become fond of saying, it's not about timing the market; it's about time in the market.

Few people are willing to invest when the stock market is down. Why would you be any different?

The stock market is going up. You start thinking, OK, this looks like the place to be. Anyone already invested glows with confidence. You don't want to miss out and invest.

You are part of a rush of buyers - including the experts - who have jumped on just as things are about to go down temporarily.

It's about now that you admit things are not going the way you would like.

You don't want to lose any more money. You sell at a loss. You have tried to buy low and sell high. Like a bad nightmare, almost exactly the opposite has happened.

MOST INVESTORS ARE TRAPPED IN A CYCLE OF FEAR AND GREED. WHEN THE MARKET GOES UP, THEY ARE DESPERATE TO RAKE IN MORE THAN THEIR NEIGHBOURS. WHEN IT FALLS, THEY BECOME CONVINCED THAT IT WILL NEVER RECOVER.

THE ECONOMIST

There are two kinds of investors, be they large or small: those who don't know where the market is headed, and those who don't know that they don't know.

WILLIAM J. BERNSTEIN, AUTHOR OF 'THE FOUR PILLARS OF INVESTING'

The odds of succeeding at stock-picking are the same as playing Russian roulette with a sixteen-shot revolver loaded with fifteen bullets! If this is your strategy, over 10 or 20 years you're going to shoot yourself in the foot. A lot.

2. The reality of buying only shares that will do well?

You'll generate more stress than wealth.

We all overestimate our ability to pick winners. Speculators use graphs, data and obsessive amounts of brainpower to find shares they believe will go up.

You don't have the patience or skill for all this. Instead, you'll hope and pray. Please may I find the goose that will lay the golden egg. The share that will turn a little money into a lot. Overnight.

Try it. You'll soon realise that picking shares is not for you.

Firstly, between R12 and R15 billion worth of transactions take place on the South African stock market every day. Do you really think your share has magically been overlooked by everyone else?

Secondly, when the market does go up, it's because of 5 or 6 shares. Even if you own another 94 shares ... sorry, no goose, no golden egg.

Picking shares is like playing the Lotto. It costs money. Winning is what dreams are made of, but in reality placing bets week after week slowly erodes your wealth.

I had no idea that fees and costs would have such a corrosive effect on my investments, I am embarrassed to say.

3. The reality of consulting an investment advisor or stockbroker?

Experts play an invaluable role in your investment life. They teach you to be prudent. They help you diversify. And they make sure you have a margin of safety. But will they help you make the most of the market? John Bogle, a man who has studied the follies of investing most of his life, suggests not.

- In the USA the best advisors lagged the performance of the market by about 40% for a six-year period.
- Using a broker will reduce your returns to about 25% of the market.
- Investors who receive frequent news updates on their stocks have earned half the returns of investors who got no news at all.

How can that be possible? Aren't these people meant to be smart? Yes, well, that's the point. These people *are* smart. Their bread and butter comes, not from investing in the market, but from fees and commissions. This is how they make a living.

Fair enough. But if you find yourself trading frequently, paying all those fees, perhaps that's why you're lagging the market by some distance.

WARNING

You may start to feel a little queasy over the next few pages.

4. The reality of putting your money in a unit trust?

Unit trusts are a truly great financial invention. They help people become part of the economy. They are simple and affordable. And they diversify your investment.

It's no surprise, then, that the unit trust industry in South Africa is huge: it's worth R660 billion.

But are unit trusts the way to make the most of the market? No, they aren't.

The reason is, unit trust managers pick shares in the hope of doing *better* than the market. And guess what? In the long run, most of them end up doing worse than the market.

They want to do better than the market to attract investors. But the costs of trying to outperform the market work against them.

In South Africa, the average unit trust investor who invested R10,000 in 1991 grew his wealth to R32,000 in 2005. The stock market would have grown the same R10,000 to R89,000 in 2005. That's 2.8 times more. It is shocking to discover that the average unit trust holder underperforms the market by a whopping 7.63 percent per annum.

MARK PAWLEY, MONEYWISE

Are unit trusts history?

Research has been done in different countries, in different decades, under different conditions, and it all reaches pretty much the same conclusions.

1. The percentage of unit trusts that fall behind the stock market increases with time

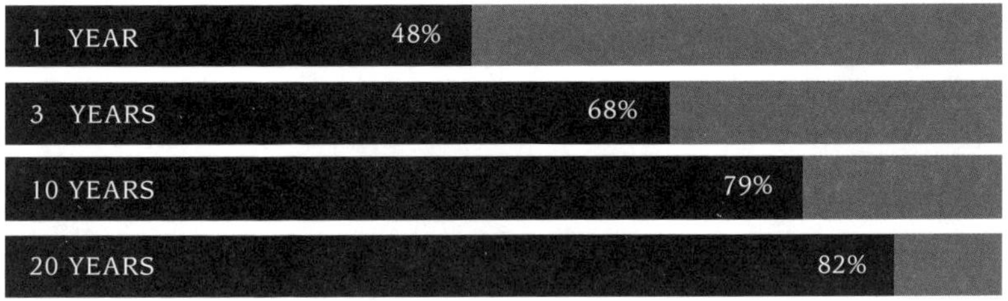

These figures don't include unit trusts that were closed because they were doing badly. Including them would, of course, make the figures worse.

There are 855 unit trusts in South Africa. Your challenge is not to find a winner, but to avoid the hundreds of laggards. How do you do that *before* you invest?

To make matters worse, the funds which have out-performed the market are likely to have a reversal of fortune and do worse than the market. Your chances of investing in a top-performing fund on the basis of its track record are close to zero.

We never employed fund managers, some of the world's most highly paid people, since we discovered their best kept secret – they could never consistently beat the stock market index.

RICHARD BRANSON

IT IS A FAILURE OF THE SYSTEM WHEN MONEY MANAGERS ARE PAID HUGE SUMS TO MOVE MONEY AROUND WHILE NOBODY BUT THE INVESTORS THEMSELVES SUFFER THE COSTS OF UNDERPERFORMANCE.

TREVOR MANUEL, MINISTER OF FINANCE

2. The average unit trust manager cannot pick shares well enough to overcome his fees and trading costs

This is not just a local phenomenon. America's S&P 500 index has outpaced 67% of large-cap general equity funds because of their management fees. An equivalent international index has outpaced 80% of actively-managed international equity funds.

3. For 20 years, the average actively-managed large-cap unit trust has underperformed the S&P 500 by almost 1.5% per year.

Does 1.5% really matter, you ask? Isn't that insignificant?

READ THIS CAREFULLY AND NEVER FORGET IT

A 1.5 percent underperformance will reduce the wealth you have in 20 years time by ... 30 percent.

The stock market could have grown your wealth to R1,767,207.90. Your unit trust, underperforming by just 1.5 percent, causes you to lose out on ... R530,162.37.

1.5 percent matters.

30%

This is the wealth you generate.

This is the bit you'll never see thanks to just 1.5%.

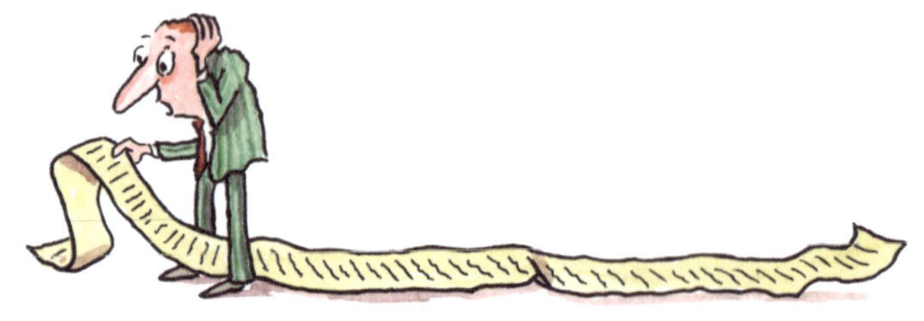

The truth is that, for the most part, fund managers have offered extremely poor value for money. Their records of outperformance are almost always followed by stretches of under-performance.

Over long periods of time, hardly any fund managers have beaten the market averages. They encourage investors, rather than spread their risks wisely or seek the best match for their future liabilities, to put their money into the most modish assets going, often just when they become overvalued. And all the while they charge their clients big fees for the privilege of losing their money … THE ECONOMIST

GREED IS THE ENEMY OF GREAT

4

The idea of doubling your wealth every 4 years 2 months takes your breath away. It's amazing.

But ... hang on a moment ... it's the *average* of the whole market. Why not invest in the market that is *above* average?

That insatiable beast lurking inside you - your greed - is speaking. Go on, it says. You can be better than average.

ACTIVE INVESTING

I want to do better than the market.
I want to beat the index.

A passively-managed ETF invests in all the shares of an index - whether they are good, bad or ugly. It delivers the performance of the index - no more, no less.

Human beings find it very hard to be average.

You'd hate to be called an average parent. Or an average child. Or an average anything.

Who wants to be average?

That's why active investing is so popular. It's what speculators do. It's what fund managers do. It's what stockbrokers do. This is their calling. The fire in their bellies.

For them, the performance of the market - far from being breathtakingly powerful - is average. Active investing is about beating the stock market. Crushing it. Making it look silly.

And you believe it's possible.

NO

BE VERY CAREFUL

This is not a game.
Do not try this at home.

In real life the risks of active investing are unforgiving. They can destroy your life.

Do not confuse yourself with a short-term trader or speculator. You may feel smart. But do the short-term, speculative ways of investing work for long-term investing? Is beating the market remotely feasible in the long run?

Q.

Why don't the smart ways work in the long run?

Either people are not aware of the harsh realities of investing in the stock market. Or, being human, they ignore them.

The First Harsh Reality
The Zero Sum Game

The first simple truth about the stock market you should get into your head now. *For every person who makes a profit, someone else makes a loss.*

When people trade shares and make money, there have to be other people who trade the same shares and lose, collectively, the same amount of money.

No amount of smartness will make this go away.

The Second Harsh Reality
Reversion to reality

Speculators can cause the share market to rise and fall by large amounts. Exuberance can make it rise irrationally and fear can make it fall terrifyingly. Emotions will lose touch with reality.

And the reality is, the long-term growth of the share market is driven almost entirely by the fortunes of the companies listed on it - and very little by emotions of the speculators trading on it.

Common sense tells you that, in the long run, the returns of the market cannot be grown by emotions. It must be grown by the returns of the companies listed on it. That's exactly the way it is.

Ow! That's gotta hurt!

The Third Harsh Reality
Costs cost. A lot.

Collectively, investors will always make what the market makes minus their costs.

Every time you buy or sell a share, it costs you money. Every time you get someone's advice, it costs you money.

Regardless of whether you are making a profit or a loss, you will pay brokerage fees, commissions, upfront costs, admin fees, annual management fees.

In 2007, the South African public paid an estimated R8,4 billion in brokerage costs. In other words, it was guaranteed that South Africans would make R8.4 billion less than the stock market, no matter whether it went up or down.

Whether it rains or shines, whether the market rises or falls, costs and fees are constantly eating away at your money. Slowly and remorselessly, they ensure you make less of the market.

Minimising costs is vital to making the most of the market.

SAINT JACK SLAYS THE DRAGON

5

If being smart so obviously doesn't make the most of the market, is it possible to invest in the market **WITHOUT** being smart?

WITHOUT picking shares?

WITHOUT timing your investment?

WITHOUT active fund managers or investment advisors?

WITHOUT all those darn costs?

When John Bogle was a student at Princeton University, he took a long, hard look at actively-managed investment funds.

He looked at their costs. He looked at the fact that they didn't do what they said they would do – outperform the market. And he realised what had to be done.

Stop trying to be smart. Stop trying to outperform the market. Focus, instead, on reducing costs and fees.

In 1976, as chairman of the Vanguard Group, he made his ideas real.

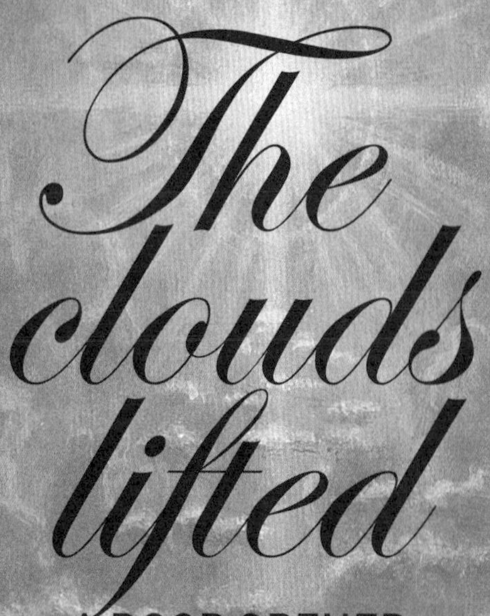
The clouds lifted
A DOOR OPENED.
A NEW WORLD
WAS REVEALED.

Saint Jack, as some investors like to call him, created the world's first index fund. The Vanguard 500 invests people's money in all 500 companies of the S&P 500 index, making no attempt to sort the winners from the losers.

Today, the Vanguard 500 is the largest investment fund in the world.

The Vanguard doesn't try to be smart. Instead, it focuses on reducing costs and fees. Because it doesn't cherry-pick shares or time its investments, the Vanguard 500 doesn't require a team of high-powered fund managers. Costs are cut to the bare minimum.

Bogle's genius was to recognize that most investors – including the managers of mutual funds – underperform the market ... Bogle's simple idea was to create a fund that would track the market. There was no longer any need for high-priced stock pickers or heavy portfolio turnover.

TIME MAGAZINE, 26 APRIL, 2004, IN A SPECIAL FEATURE ON THE 100 MOST INFLUENTIAL PEOPLE IN THE WORLD. (WHICH INCLUDES NELSON MANDELA, BY THE WAY.)

An ETF's rock-bottom costs and fees give it an insurmountable advantage over actively-managed, actively-charged unit trusts.

"I can make the case with great simplicity. An investor with $10,000 at the start of 1969 who invested in a Standard & Poor's 500 Stock Index Fund would have had a portfolio worth $422,000 by 2006, assuming that all dividends were reinvested. A second investor who instead purchased shares in the average actively-managed

fund would have seen his investment grow to $284,000. The difference is dramatic. Through March 31, 2006, the index investor was ahead by $138,000, an amount almost 50% greater than the final stake of the average investor in a actively-managed fund."

BURTON MALKIEL. WHO IN HIS BOOK, 'A RANDOM WALK DOWN WALL STREET', ENJOYS POINTING OUT THAT A CHIMPANZEE THROWING DARTS AT THE STOCK MARKET PAGE WILL HAVE AS MUCH LUCK PICKING SHARES AS A WALL STREET ANALYST.

DON'T LOOK F
BUY THE

R THE NEEDLE AYSTACK

JOHN BOGLE

IT'S NOT ABOUT HOW SMART YOU CAN BE.

You don't ...

- Rush into the market because everyone thinks it's going up.
- Spend hours sifting through thousands of companies, looking for some undiscovered gem that is about shoot up - maybe.
- Subscribe to newsletters, read investment columns or even bother with the market report on your way home from work.
- Pay the brokerage and tax on all sorts of gambles that may or may not pay off.
- Go in search of unit trusts that have done a stellar job over the last 12 months, hoping they'll repeat their performance over the next 12.
- Pay the actively-managed costs and fees of a unit trust that can erode your wealth in stomach-churning amounts.
- You don't, in short, try to outsmart the market.

IT'S ABOUT HOW WEALTHY YOU CAN BE.

Instead ...

- You invest in the most powerful companies on the stock exchange. All of them. Without wondering which will do better than the rest.
- You ensure that you own the 5 or 6 companies on the 5 or 6 days of the year when the market goes up significantly.
- You capture every cent of their growth.
- You reinvest every dividend you earn.
- You let the growth of your wealth compound itself, month after month, year after year.
- You keep your costs - and your taxes - to the bare minimum.

Make no mistake about it, embracing the concept of using index mutual funds can be a life-altering event

...

All your life you read the popular financial press, listened to market experts on TV, and went with a few of your stockbroker's recommendations

...

Once you understand the philosophy behind an index fund strategy, your beliefs about investing will change forever. RICHARD A. FERRI

ETFs FOR SOUTH AFRICAN INVESTORS

And now for some really dry figures that will convince you that ETFs are the new, big thing.

Today, around the world, one quarter of all money invested in collective investment schemes (unit trusts, index funds and ETFs) is invested in passively-managed index funds and ETFs.

Even the large financial institutions - with all their skills and resources - invest between 25 and 40% of their funds in passively-managed funds. Since 2002, most passive investing has gone into ETFs. With good reason.

- Their low costs and fees.
- Their transparency - unlike a unit trust, you know exactly what you are invested in and what your investment is worth at any moment in the day.
- Their simplicity - you can buy and sell them as easily as you buy and sell shares (not that you're a speculator).
- Their ability to defer taxation - ETFs are not charged capital gains tax on their capital gains.
- Their comprehensiveness - if a company in the index stops performing or if another should rise to prominence, the fund is updated. It's like being told which companies to invest in - for free.

By mid-2007, $700 billion had been invested in 953 ETFs on 41 stock exchanges around the world. That figure is expected to pass $2 trillion by 2011.

The broad-market ETFs

ETF	What it does	TER (basis points)	How to invest
Satrix 40	It invests your money in the 40 largest companies on the JSE, which account for 95 percent of the trading on the JSE, by tracking the FTSE/JSE Top 40 index. The companies are diversified across mining, consumer goods and services, banking, industry and manufacturing, telecommunications, oil and gas, insurance and retail.	45	The Satrix Investment Plan 086 110 0670 International +27 11 561 6890 www.satrix.co.za
db x-trackers FTSE 100 Index ETF	It invests your money in the 100 largest UK companies on the London Stock Exchange, tracking the FTSE 100 index.	114	Hotline 0861 111288 www.dbxtrackers.co.za +27 11 775 7994
db x-trackers DJ Eurostoxx 50 Index ETF	It invests your money in 50 blue-chip companies in the Eurozone by tracking the Dow Jones Euro STOXX 50 index.	114	As above
db x-trackers USA Index ETF	It invests your money is 600 companies in the USA's economy, in essence tracking the USA share markets.	114	As above
db x-trackers MSCI Japan Index ETF	It invests your money in 400 companies in the Japanese economy.	114	As above
db x-trackers MSCI World Index ETF	It invests your money in 1,900 companies in 23 developed economies around the world.	114	As above
Satrix SWIX Top 40	It tracks the FTSE/JSE SWIX Top 40, an index of the same 40 companies that Satrix 40 invests in, reweighted to reduce the effects of foreign participation on price volatility and exchange-rate fluctuations. It is suited to large institutional investors.	45	The Satrix Investment Plan 086 110 0670 International +27 11 561 6890 www.satrix.co.za

These are classic ETFs. They are practical, simple and cost-effective ways to invest in the wealth-generating companies of any economy - South African, British, European or Japanese.

TER stands for Total Expense Ratio, the all-important measure of your costs. The TER is the total running cost of a fund (management fees, trading fees, legal fees, etc) expressed as a percentage of the fund's total assets. The smaller the TER, the better. Basis points (bps) are one-hundredths of 1%. 100bps is equal to 1%.

Compared to the figures opposite, the TER for the average South African large-cap equity unit trust is 127 basis points.

Around the world, the picture is pretty much the same.
Annual expenses for ETFs : 7 to 111 basis points
Traditional mutual funds: 39 to 191 basis points

The ETFs that invest in sectors of the stock market

ETF	What it does	TER (basis points)	How to invest
Satrix FINI	It invests your money in South Africa's largest banks, the main long-term and short-term insurance companies, and other financial and property companies by tracking the FTSE/JSE Fini 15 index. It is suited for investment in companies that benefit from an expanding banking and financial system, and the funding of a growing economy.	45	The Satrix Investment Plan 086 110 0670 International +27 11 561 6890 www.satrix.co.za
Satrix INDI	It invests your money in the 25 largest industrial, retail and manufacturing companies on the JSE by tracking the FTSE/JSE INDI Industrial 25 index. The Satrix INDI is suited for investment in large local companies with their emphasis on job and infrastructure provision and the 2010 World Cup.	45	As above
Satrix RESI	It invests your money solely in 20 resources companies - mining and resource-based companies - by tracking the FTSE/JSE Resources 20 index. Ideal if you would like to invest in companies that will benefit from a global demand for commodities, while hedging your investments against a possible weakening of the Rand.	45	As above
NewGold	These Gold Bullion Debentures enable you to invest, not in a diversity of companies, but in gold bullion itself, allowing you to benefit from the performance of gold as a long-term investment or as a Rand hedge.	30	The Investment Plan 0860 122 122 Absa Stockbrokers 011 647 0817 www.absa.co.za

These ETFs focus on niche sectors of the market. If you believe that a particular sector of the economy will do better than the overall market, then you will use one of these ETFs to diversify your investment simply and cost-effectively across the largest companies in that sector.

While the ETFs remain passive investments, your decision to focus on a particular sector and time your investing makes you an active investor.

The ETFs that try to outperform the stock market

It's that story of not wanting to be average. Part of you wants to be a passive investor, part of you wants to outperform the market.

ETFs now track what are called enhanced indices. They are concocted by experts who believe that indices made up by size are not the way to make the most of the market.

Their reasoning goes like this. If a company is overvalued, it will be over-represented in the index; similarly, if a company is undervalued it will be under-represented in the index. When an overvalued company's share price returns to its true value, you are over-exposed to the decline. Similarly, when an undervalued company rises to its true value, you are under-exposed to the rise.

Enhanced indices - instead of looking at companies by size - look at companies' fundamentals (their sales, cash flow or dividends) in the hope of providing an index that will do better than that most unacceptable of qualities - the average.

These ETFs are no longer what John Bogle envisaged when he created the index fund. They are no longer synonymous with a passive, long-term investment in the economy.

Be careful. They are less diversified, so they carry more risk. They require more management, so their fees are higher. Their portfolios will be turned over more frequently, so their costs are higher.

ETF	What it does	TER (basis points)	How to invest
Satrix DIVI	This ETF provides investment in the 30 companies on the JSE expected to pay higher than average dividends. It will appeal to investors seeking a high income portfolio.	45	The Satrix Investment Plan 086 110 0670 International +27 11 561 6890 www.satrix.co.za
Zshares RandPlay	This ETF allows you to invest in companies that will benefit from sustained Rand/Dollar strength by tracking the RandPlay Index developed by Investec Bank and calculated by FTSE/JSE.	Cannot be accurately determined as the fund is less than six months old.	Contact Investec Bank Limited Zshares@ investec.co.za 0860 zshares (0860 974273)
Zshares RandHedge	It allows you focus your investment on South African companies that will benefit from sustained Rand/Dollar weakness. It tracks the RandHedge Index developed by Investec Bank and calculated by FTSE/JSE.	As above	As above
NewRand	The ETF enables you to invest in the growth potential of the top 10 South African Rand-hedge stocks. It replicates the performance of the NewRand Index. The index, created by Absa Corporate and Merchant Bank, calculated by FTSE and the JSE, seeks to maximise a long-term correlation with the Rand/USD exchange rate.	92	The Investment Plan 0860 122 122 Absa Stockbrokers 011 647 0817 www.absa.co.za
eRAFI	It tracks the eRAFI™ Overall SA Index, enabling you to invest in 40 South African companies chosen, not for their market size, but for their potential to provide smoother and higher-compounding long-term returns than those of the Top 40 Index.	Max 80 with sliding scale applicable. (TER supplied after 1 month's trading.)	As above. www.newfunds. co.za

MAKE THE MOST OF THE MARKET

YOUR JOB
IS TO
SQUEEZE
THE MOST
OUT OF THE
MARKET

This is not a Get Rich Quickly book. There is no such thing. The stock market is a powerful ally to any long-term investor. But don't ever be tempted to outperform it. Reducing costs is a far more valuable pursuit.

That's what index-tracking ETFs do. Even for the investor with a few hundred Rands every month.

The South African stock market has doubled in value every 4 years 2 months for the past 20 years. That is no guarantee it will do the same for the next 20 years. It may grow less. Or it may grow more. No one knows.

Whatever it does, here are well-known principles to help you squeeze the most out of its growth.

Howzit?

1. The miracle of compounding

There is one secret to getting rich: Get rich slowly. Be patient. Earn a return. Then earn a return on your return. And then earn returns on the returns of your return.

Invest R1,000 and one year of growth at 20% gives you growth of R200. But ten years of growth won't give you ten times that, or R2,000. It will give you growth of R5,191.74.

This is the miracle of compounding.

That's how R1,000 invested 20 years ago on the South African stock exchange became R25,243.18

The longer you invest, the wealthier compounding helps you become. No wonder Albert Einstein called compounding 'the greatest mathematical discovery of all time.'

Compounding is also why it's so important to minimise your costs and fees. Every Rand that you pay out now is not only a Rand that you don't have, it's also a Rand you don't have working for you. Every time you pay tax, not only do you lose that money; you also lose the chance of that money making money for you. Just as R1,000 can turn into R25,243.18, so every R1,000 you don't have, won't turn into R25,243.18 later on.

AMAZING!
Yes!
CHEAP!
ONLY!
LOOK!
SPECIAL
Sale!

2. Rand-cost averaging

Which way is the stock market going? Is it going up or going down? Is it the right time or the wrong time to invest?

Rand-cost averaging does away with all this worry. You invest the same amount every month, year after year, whether the market is up or down.

When the market is down, Great! It's like being at a sale. You buy more for less. And you won't worry that you're investing too much when the market looks risky.

When the market is up, Great! Your investments are up. Your preset amount buys you fewer shares, preventing you from over-investing when the market, no matter how strong it looks, may be poised to go down.

The market can fluctuate all it wants. Experts can pull their hair out as it continues to baffle and bewilder them. You have relegated your investment decisions to a debit-order. Out of sight, out of mind. It's like paying off your car – but it's a better long-term investment.

THE CRASH OF 1929

There's no greater test of Rand-cost or Dollar-cost averaging than the infamous crash of 1929. What would have happened if you had deliberately invested a set amount every month through one of the darker times in American history?

According to Ibbotson Associates, the leading financial research firm, if you had invested $12,000 in the Standard & Poor's 500 stock index at the beginning of September 1929, 10 years later you would have had only $7,223 left.

But if you had started with a paltry $100 and simply invested another $100 every single month, then by August 1939, your money would have grown to $15,571! That's the power of disciplined buying - even in the face of the Great Depression and the worst bear market of all time. JASON ZWEIG

THE STOCK MARKET
IS NOT ALWAYS GOING
TO BEHAVE THE WAY
YOU WOULD LIKE

3. Have a margin of safety

The market will fluctuate all the time. Occasionally it will fall heavily. Or it will stay down longer than you could wish. You know that.

Even when the stock market is at its most positive, something totally unexpected can change all that. Planes fly into buildings, birds get flu ...

You can't predict these things. But you can be prepared for them.

Margin of safety. Warren Buffett, arguably the world's greatest investor, calls them the three most important words in all of investing. Never become a forced seller: selling when your investments are down because you need the money.

You must be able to weather periods of a few years when the stock market doesn't rise. Know this now. If you can't handle it, don't invest.

THE LONGER YOU INVEST IN THE STOCK MARKET, THE LESS RISKY IT BECOMES

THE LONGER YOU INVEST IN THE STOCK MARKET, THE MORE RESPONSIBLE YOUR DECISION BECOMES

4. Is the stock market risky or responsible?

Many people think the stock market is risky because it can go down at any time. Compare it with the bank where your money starts earning interest the moment you make the deposit.

The bank looks a lot less risky. But is it?

Over the long term, keeping your money in the bank is irresponsible. Inflation erodes its value. Your purchasing power declines. You're doing yourself, your retirement and your children no favours at all.

A fixed deposit investment over the 20 year period 1986 – 2005, assuming a tax rate of 40 percent and zero withdrawals, would have declined in value. So what was the point? Risk reduction? It just doesn't make sense. MARK PAWLEY, MONEYWISE

Yes, the stock market fluctuates all the time. If you're investing for the short term and you're forced to sell at a loss, you have every reason to call yourself irresponsible.

But remember the graph on page 18. The longer you invest, the less risky the stock market becomes. And the more responsible your investment becomes.

BOOM!

5. Don't panic

The stock market has survived a lot more than the crisis it's going through right now. It has weathered world wars, apartheid, world isolation, sanctions, the bursting of the dot.com bubble ...

The reason any downturn looms large, keeping you awake at night, is that human beings feel pain far more deeply than they feel pleasure. Pleasure is normal.

A crisis may look like the end of the world. In reality, the only crisis is the emotional one building inside you. And it will only occur if you lose control of your emotions and sell at a loss.

6. In praise of the couch potato

Lethargy bordering on sloth remains the best investment style. The correct holding period for the stock market is forever. WARREN BUFFETT

In praise of the investor who invests his time in pursuits other than the stock market. In children, in sport, in friends, in hobbies, in a career, in cooking, in taking the dogs for a walk, in DIY, in watching TV, in marvelling at the world.

By being a passive investor, you will do better than 80% of investors around the world over the next few decades. And you will do it by having as little as possible to do with the stock market.

Being passive sounds all wrong. It sounds lazy. It sounds like you're not interested in your investments. It even sounds like you don't deserve to creatc wealth.

But if you want to make the most of the market, being passive is the smartest thing you will ever do.

Sources

PAGES 3 - 7 AND 18

The statistics are supplied by Mark Pawley of Moneywise for the period 1988 - 2007. Gross geometric rates of return, using R1000 invested at the beginning of the period, gross:
Equities: 17.52%
Property (without rental income - primary residence - and no adjustment to the growth for house maintenance or financing costs/insurance): 13.19%
Bonds: 9.20%
Inflation: 8.38%
Fixed Deposit (income reduced for 40% income tax): 7.46%

For a great study of how shares have outperformed other investments, read Siegel, J.J. 2008. *Stocks for the long run,* Fourth Edition. McGraw-Hill.

PAGE 24

1. The top 40 shares account for approximately 98 percent of the stock market's return for this period
2. Costs, as detailed later, play a vital role in making the most of the market

PAGE 26

Source: Ferri, R.A. 2007. *All About Index Funds,* Second Edition. McGraw Hill: 42. In the 1950s, researchers - some of whom went on to win the Nobel Prize in Economics - discovered that the most efficient portfolio of shares was the market itself. Earlier, in 1933, Alfred Cowles published a report on the futility of using Wall Street research to beat the market. In 1973, Burton Malkiel (quoted elsewhere in our book) wrote his irreverent *A Random Walk Down Wall Street,* noting that actively-managed funds did not keep up with the market. And in 1975, Charles Ellis published an acclaimed article, *The Loser's Game,* reporting that in the previous decade 85 percent of institutional investors had not performed as well as the S&P 500 index.

PAGE 41

Malkiel, B.G. 2007. *A Random Walk Down Wall Street.* Norton Books: 172. Burton Malkiel quotes an academic study by Professors Richard Woodward and Jess Chua of the University of Calgary.

PAGE 43

Other people's money, A survey of asset management, *The Economist,* July 5th - 11th 2003. Also the source of other quotations from The Economist.

PAGE 44

The analogy seems to have been banging around for a number of years, but was supplied Roland Rousseau, Director of Quantitative Investment Strategy research at Deutsche Securities.

PAGE 47

The first two of these eye-opening statistics come from Bogle, J.C. 2007. *The Little Book of Common Sense Investing.* John Wiley and Sons, Inc. The third statistic is from Malkiel, B.G. *A Random Walk Down Wall Street.*

PAGE 49 AND 51

Statistics about South African unit trust funds come from the Association for Collective Investments, quoted in *Business Day,* Johannesburg, 18 July 2008.

PAGE 50
Source: Pawley, M. 2007. *Moneywise Investment Returns*. Moneywise.co.za
Mark Pawley became a certified financial planner and set up his own investment company after he became disappointed by the "utterly inappropriate and downright poor advice dispensed by hopelessly inept financial advisors."

PAGE 51
Percent of large-cap equity funds outperformed by the S&P 500 for period ended Dec 31, 2005. Malkiel, B.G. 2007. *A Random Walk Down Wall Street*. Norton Books: 268

PAGE 52
Richard Branson quoted in Other people's money, A survey of asset management, *The Economist*, July 5th - 11th 2003

PAGE 53
Bogle, J.C. 2007. *The Little Book of Common Sense Investing*. John Wiley and Sons, Inc: 131 and 132

PAGE 69
JSE annual value of trades (2007) - R2,800bn
Brokerage (0,3%) on trades - R8,4bn

PAGES 78 AND 79
Malkiel, B.G. 2007. *A Random Walk Down Wall Street*. Norton Books: 15

PAGES 80 AND 81
Bogle, J.C. 2007. *The Little Book of Common Sense Investing*. John Wiley and Sons, Inc: 78

PAGE 85
Ferri, R.A. 2007. *All About Index Funds*: xii
Richard A. Ferri was a stockbroker, an investment consultant and a commodities trader before he stopped trying to beat the market.

PAGE 89
Source: *The Financial Times Weekly Review of the Fund Management Industry*, November 5, 2007

PAGES 90 TO 95
Facts about the various ETFs come from fund managers and their websites. Care has been taken to get the details correct, but some details will change over time.

PAGE 105
The example comes from Jason Zweig's commentary on the original text of Graham, B. 1973, *The Intelligent Investor*, Fourth Edition. Collins Business Essentials: 131. His source is, in turn, spreadsheet data provided courtesy of Ibbotson Associates. It was not possible to buy the entire S&P 500 index until 1976.

PAGE 113
Warren Buffett is quoted by Malkiel, B.G. 2007. *A Random Walk Down Wall Street*. Norton Books: 241